GW00359536

Welcome to the 2C   of Ireland's Blue
Book. We are a unique association comprising the
country's finest country manor houses, historic
hotels, castles and restaurants. No two properties
are the same, each offering an enchanting and
unique atmosphere.

If your choice is golf or beautiful scenery; mountains to climb;
rivers and lakes to fish; miles and miles of golden beaches, a Blue
Book property is the perfect choice. Other activities available at
some properties include cookery lessons; garden courses, spa and
equestrian pursuits. The Blue Book also includes five of Dublin's
finest restaurants for those wishing to dine in our capital city.

The properties are all independently owned and reflect a diversity
of style and character.

We look forward to welcoming you in 2015.

C. Dundon

Catherine Dundon
President of Ireland's Blue Book

IRISCHE LANDHÄUSER UND RESTAURANTS

Hinter dem Namen **Ireland's Blue Book** verbirgt sich ein exklusiver Zusammenschluss irischer Gastbetriebe, die in einzigartigen Land- und Herrenhäusern, Schlössern und Gourmetrestaurants untergebracht sind. Die Häuser der Blue Book-Mitglieder sind ideal für den anspruchsvollen Gast und bieten traditionelle irische Gastfreundschaft, erstklassige Unterbringung und Gourmetküche inmitten der anmutigen Schönheit der ländlichen Idylle Irlands.

CASAS DE CAMPO Y RESTAURANTES DE IRLANDA

Ireland's Blue Book es un exclusivo Grupo que reúne a las principales casas solariegas, hoteles históricos, castillos y restaurantes de Irlanda. Los establecimientos que se presentan en el Blue Book colmarán las expectativas de los visitantes más exigentes, atraídos por la serena belleza de la Irlanda rural ya sea en busca de hospitalidad tradicional, alojamiento o gastronomía de calidad.

RISTORANTI E DIMORE DI CAMPAGNA IRLANDESI

Ireland's Blue Book è un'associazione esclusiva che riunisce le dimore di campagna, gli hotel storici, i castelli e i ristoranti più belli del paese. Gli edifici descritti nel Blue Book non potranno fare a meno di attirare l'attenzione dei visitatori più esigenti in cerca di accoglienza tradizionale, ospitalità dagli standard elevati e cucina squisita nella serena bellezza della campagna irlandese.

RELAIS DE CAMPAGNE ET RESTAURANTS D'IRLANDE

Ireland's Blue Book est une association exceptionnelle qui rassemble les plus beaux manoirs, hôtels à caractère historique, châteaux et restaurants du pays. Les établissements présentés dans le Blue Book séduiront les visiteurs exigeants, à la recherche d'une hospitalité traditionnelle et raffinée, d'un hébergement de qualité et d'une cuisine savoureuse, au coeur de la beauté paisible d'une Irlande rurale.

魅力的なカントリーハウス・ホテルとレストラン

「アイルランド・ブルーブック」には、アイルランドで指折りのカントリー・ハウス、城、レストランが加盟しています。静かで美しいアイルランドの自然のなかで、伝統的に名高いアイルランド流「おもてなし」が体験できる、宿泊施設、レストランをお探しの方に、最適の場をご紹介しています。

HOW TO BOOK A BLUE BOOK HOUSE

Simply log onto the Ireland's Blue Book website and make your reservation/booking.

www.irelandsbluebook.com

Perhaps you are more comfortable dealing with a person rather than booking online. In this instance please contact the houses directly; they would love to hear from you. At the bottom of each page you will find the proprietor's name, address, telephone, email, website and fax numbers.

Reservations can also be made through your travel agent.

Reservation Agents in North America and Canada, please call

USA/Canada Toll Free 800 323 5463

Contact details
Ireland's Blue Book
7-8 Mount Street Crescent
Dublin 2, Ireland

T +353 (0) 1 676 9914
USA/Canada Toll Free 800 323 5463
E mail@irelandsbluebook.com
www.irelandsbluebook.com

AHERNE'S TOWNHOUSE LUXURY INN & SEAFOOD RESTAURANT

Open fires and the warmest of welcomes await you in this family run hotel in the historic walled port of Youghal. Rooms are spacious and stylishly furnished. The famous Seafood Bar and Restaurant specialises in the freshest of Seafood (Lobster, Oysters, Crab, Prawns, Black Sole, Monkfish & Turbot) our bar is renowned for its friendliness; you can enjoy a chat with the locals along with your Guinness and Seafood. Gluten-free meals served for 30 years. Available for Intimate Weddings /Private Parties. Civil Marriage approved.

Local attractions: Walking, Swimming, Seaweed Baths, Horse Riding, Golfing, Sea Angling, Kayaking, Greyhound Racing, Jameson Heritage Centre, Fota Wildlife Park, Ardmore Cliff Walk, Blarney Castle, Waterford Crystal and Lismore Castle.

Awards include:
Listed in the country's **top** 20 best Pubs in **Hot Press** Best of Ireland 2014
Guardian Newspaper – 'One of the best breakfasts in Ireland'

A Blue Book Voucher – complimentary upgrade where possible.

Bedrooms **12**   Guesthouse ★ ★ ★ ★

Aherne's, 163 North Main Street, Youghal, Co.Cork
T +353 (0)24 92424
F +353 (0)24 93633
info@ahernes.net
www.ahernes.com

Proprietor: The FitzGibbon Family
Open all year – except 4 days at Christmas.
Bed & Breakfast from €55 – €75 pps.
Single from €80 – €120.
Dinner 6.00pm to 9.30pm from €30.00.
Bar Food Service available Noon – 10pm daily.
Guide dogs welcome.
Small dogs by arrangement.

How to find:
Cork: 30 mins. (N25) Direction Rosslare.
Rosslare: 1.45hrs (N25).
Dublin: Take the N7 then the M7 onto the M9 to Waterford then take the N25 West to Youghal. 2.30hrs.

GPS coordinates
Lat: 51.957031634671
Long: -7.8518871130346

ARDTARA

Ardtara is an elegantly restored 19th century mansion, **situated at the centre of Northern Ireland in the Sperrin Mountains region and within 45 minutes of the North Antrim Coast, the Giant's Causeway, Derry/ Londonderry and Belfast.**

In fact, every scenic attraction in Northern Ireland north of Belfast, plus all airports and Royal Portrush, Portstewart & Castlerock links' golf are all within 60 minutes of Ardtara *(source: Google Maps).*

Ardtara is honoured to be included in **National Geographic Traveler Magazine's** 'Best Places to Stay in Britain and Ireland 2010' and was previously named 'Most Romantic Hotel of the Year' by the Automobile Association.

Ardtara has nine en-suite bedrooms with king beds, owner-collected antiques, 14 original working fireplaces and award winning Irish cuisine.

Bedrooms **9**   **Listed Heritage Property**

**Ardtara Country House & Restaurant,
8 Gorteade Road, Upperlands,
Co. L'Derry BT46 5SA**
T +44 (0)28 796 44490
info@ardtara.com
www.ardtara.com

Manager: Valerie M. Ferson
Closed 25 and 26 December.
Bed & Full Irish Breakfast from £49.50 – £70 pps.
Garden Room Supplement £10.
Single Supplement £15.
Dinner 7.00pm – 9.00pm à la carte.
Complimentary Wi-Fi on ground floor.
Dinner available to non-residents by reservation.
Private Dining Room available if requested.

How to find:
Take M2/M22/A6 north toward Derry/Londonderry.
7 miles past the Castledawson roundabout, take
A29 to Maghera. Continue on A29 towards
Coleraine for three miles out of Maghera to the
right turn on to B75. Proceed one mile into
Upperlands. Ardtara sign is on the left towards
the end of the village.

GPS coordinates
N 54.88297
W -6.636611

BALLYFIN DEMESNE

COUNTRY HOUSE HOTEL

Set at the foot of the Slieve Bloom Mountains just over an hour from Dublin, Ballyfin has long been admired as the most lavish Regency mansion in Ireland. It is a place of history and romance, of tranquillity and great natural beauty.

Activities include boating and fishing on the lake, biking, horse-riding, picnics, exploring the 600 acre estate, swimming pool and fitness centre, spa treatments, wine and whiskey tasting and feasting on fine food.

It is the perfect place for a break from the stresses of the modern world and provides discretion and privacy like few other destinations.

Awards include:
Garden Trophy Relais & Chateaux 2014
Andrew Harper – **International Travel** – 100 Best Hotels
   and Resorts in the World 2013
Robb Report – Best of the Best 2012 – The World's Best New Resort.
Tatler Travel Guide – Top 101 Hotels Worldwide.

Bedrooms **20**   Hotel ★ ★ ★ ★ ★

Ballyfin Demesne, Ballyfin, Co.Laois
T +353 (0)57 875 5866
reservations@ballyfin.com
www.ballyfin.com

General Manager: Damien Bastiat
Rates:
Single: From €580 Full Board
Double: From €915 Full Board
Suite: From €1,350 Full Board
Rate includes: Irish breakfast, lunch, dinner, all teas and coffees, soft drinks, pre-dinner drinks reception, laundry service and most on-site activities and gratuities.

How to find:
Ballyfin is located 10 minutes drive from Junction 18 of the M7 motorway. Leave the motorway at junction 18 signposted Tullamore and Mountrath. Follow signs for Mountrath, on entering Mountrath turn right at the traffic lights/T-junction. Continue along this road to Ballyfin for approx 7.5km and you will reach the entrance gate on the left hand side signposted Ballyfin. Press the intercom at the gate for reception.

GPS coordinates
Latitude 53' 03'.425N
Longitude 007' 25'.896W

BALLYMALOE HOUSE

A family-run country house hotel famous for its outstanding hospitality and superb food. Most produce comes from the farm and is sourced locally.

The 17th century house built onto a Norman keep is nestled in a 400 acre estate in rural east Cork. Located minutes from the breathtaking south coast and twenty miles from the historic city of Cork. Bedrooms range from elegant and airy to charming and cosy.

Facilities include a small golf course, tennis court and croquet lawn. Members of the family run the Cookery School nearby. The Grainstore provides the ideal venue for conferences, private parties and cultural events. Self catering cottages are also available.

Awards include:
Food and Wine Magazine "One of Irelands Top 10 restaurants"
Fodor's Travel Top 10 Hotels with hands on food experience
Georgina Campbell Guide best breakfast in Ireland 2012

Bedrooms **29** incl. courtyard rooms   Guesthouse ★ ★ ★ ★

Ballymaloe House, Shanagarry, Co.Cork
T +353 (0)21 465 2531
F +353 (0)21 465 2021
res@ballymaloe.ie
www.ballymaloe.ie

Proprietor: The Allen Family
Closed 24, 25, 26 December. 8 Jan. – 8 Feb.
Bed & Breakfast per person sharing.
Low season €95 – €120
High season €120 – €150.
Service charge optional.
Dinner €70, from 7.00 – 9.30pm.
All major credit cards accepted.
Children welcome.

How to find:
From Cork take N25 east. Then take R630 and R631. We are two miles beyond Cloyne on the Ballycotton road. From Waterford take N25 west to Castlemartyr. In Ladysbridge take care to follow signs to Cloyne, we are two miles from Ladysbridge on the Cloyne Road.

GPS coordinates
N 5551.88 W 00804.50
2.29 SSW Castlemartyr

BARBERSTOWN CASTLE

Formerly the home of Eric Clapton and welcoming visitors for over 800 years, visitors to Barberstown will experience a very relaxing and welcoming Castle while enjoying great food, good wines, open log fires, luxury and exceptional personal service.

Use this unique Historic 13th Century Irish Castle as the ideal base from which to visit Dublin and the East Coast of Ireland. Enjoy 30 minutes carefree driving from or to Dublin Airport and 30 minutes from all the sites to visit in Dublin City Centre.

Essential Day Trips for your Vacation – Irish National Stud and Japanese Gardens. Drive to the Garden of Ireland in Wicklow visiting Russborough, Glendalough and Powerscourt. Newgrange (5,000 year old Megalithic site) and The Rock of Cashel are great day trips.

Awards include:
Best Historic Hotel of Europe CASTLE 2014 award

Bedrooms **55 Ensuite**   Hotel ★ ★ ★ ★

**Barberstown Castle, Straffan,
Co.Kildare**
T +353 (0)1 628 8157
F +353 (0)1 627 7027
info@barberstowncastle.ie
www.barberstowncastle.ie

Proprietor: Kenneth Healy
Open all year except three days Christmas,
January and February
Bed & Breakfast Rates: €75 – €125 pps
and €52.00 single room supplement.
Dinner: Table d'Hôte Menu available.
Lunch: Tea Rooms open daily 10.00am – 8.30pm.

GDS Codes:
HE DUBBCH, HE 29023, HE 30473, HE DUBBC

How to find:
Leave the airport and take the exit for the M50
South Bound. Leave the M50 at exit #7 (M4) and
continue on the N4/M4 westward. Leave the M4
at Exit/Junction 7 (Straffan/Maynooth) and take
the R407 to Straffan. (30 minutes - all Motorway).
Onward Journey: Because the Castle is minutes
from the M1, M50, M4 and M7
motorways, it is the most perfect
starting point, or final evening, on
your Blue Book tour of Ireland.
This Castle is easy to Find
but hard to Leave!

In this Georgian country house standing at the head of Dunmanus Bay, everything revolves around the courtyard. Finely restored with cobbled paths, shrubs and flowers, its 250 year old stone outbuildings contain four beautiful guest apartments as well as the restaurant, with its magnificent dining room.

Blairscove Restaurant is best known for its buffet style starters and scrumptious desserts.

The elegant setting, the pretty courtyard and the landscaped gardens make it an ideal venue for intimate weddings.

Irish Times — 'Blairscove Restaurant has one of the most beautiful settings of any restaurant'

Sunday Times 2011: Best Restaurant with Rooms in Ireland.

AA 2 rosettes 2014.

One Fab Day 100 best wedding venues 2014.

Bedrooms **4 courtyard suites, 1 cottage in the grounds**

Blairscove House, Durrus near Bantry, Co.Cork
T +353 (0)27 61127
mail@blairscove.ie
www.blairscove.ie

Proprietor: Philippe & Sabine De Mey
Restaurant: Open from March 20 to Oct 25
Tuesday to Saturday 7.00pm – 9.30pm.
3 course table d'Hôte menu €58.00
2 course table d'Hôte menu €46.00
Accommodation: Open from 14 March to 28 Oct.
Bed & Breakfast €75 – €130 mid-week.
Friday and Saturday €110 – €130.
Single supplement €30.
Self catering cottage available.
Major credit cards accepted.

How to find: Coming from Durrus follow the R591 to Crook haven. After 1.5 miles you'll see the blue gate on the right hand side. Cork airport: 1 hr 15 mins.

GPS coordinates
51 degrees 36' 33" N
9 degrees 32' 18" W

BUSHMILLS INN HOTEL

The Bushmills Inn is situated in an enviable location a stone's throw from Royal Portrush Golf Club, The Giant's Causeway and Dunluce Castle. Roaring peat fires, nooks and crannies and a secret library set the tone.

In the bar, still lit by gas light, try a glass of malt from the hotel's private cask and sample the finest North Antrim produce in the AA Rosette restaurant.

Whether you wish to linger by the fire, enjoy afternoon tea on the garden courtyard, partake in water sports, hike in unspoilt countryside or play golf on some of Ireland's finest courses Bushmills Inn is the ideal location.

Awards include:
2013 Good Eating Guide Winner of Best Restaurant in Ulster.

Bedrooms **41**   Specialist accommodation **Historic Building**   Hotel ★ ★ ★ ★

Bushmills Inn Hotel, 9 Dunluce Road, Bushmills, Co.Antrim, BT57 8QG
T + 44(0)28 207 33000
mail@bushmillsinn.com
www.bushmillsinn.com

Proprietor: Alan Dunlop
Hotel Manager: Alan Walls
Open all year Monday to Sunday.
Restaurant open all day: 12 noon to 9.30,
dinner 6pm to 9.30pm Stg£30.
B&B: Low Season: Oct – Mar £64 – £134 pps
High Season: April – Sept £89 – £199 pps
All bedrooms non-smoking.
Credit Cards: Amex, Mastercard, Visa.

How to find:
From Belfast follow the M2 north to Ballymena then A26 to Ballymoney. At the roundabout take the third exit onto B62 heading to Portrush/Bushmills, turn right onto Priestland Road (B17) then right onto Dunluce Road (A2). The Bushmills Inn will be on the left.

GPS coordinates
N 55 12' 25.64"
W 6 31' 26.63"

CAMPAGNE RESTAURANT

Campagne restaurant in Kilkenny city opened in 2008. The emphasis has been to serve food based on high-quality seasonal produce with French influences in a relaxed and comfortable dining area.

Located under the old railway arches on Gas House Lane, Campagne boasts a stylish interior featuring oak flooring, curved banquette leather seating and modern paintings depicting rural life by Kilkenny artist Catherine Barron.

Campagne has been awarded many prestigious awards on a national and international level, most notably one Michelin star status in September 2013.

At Campagne we have a passionately held philosophy that supports and showcases the very best of quality food and wine producers.

Campagne Restaurant
5 The Arches, Gas House Lane, Kilkenny
T +353 (0)56 777 2858
info@campagne.ie www.campagne.ie

Proprietors: Garrett Byrne & Brid Hannon
Opening hours:
Closed Sunday nights and all day Monday
Lunch: Friday and Saturday 12.30pm – 2.30pm
Sunday Lunch: 12.30pm – 3.00pm
Early Bird: Tuesday – Thursday 6pm – 7pm
(5.30pm – 6pm on Fridays and Saturdays)
Dinner: Tuesday – Saturday 6pm – 10pm,
Open Sunday nights on Bank Holidays, closed on
Tuesday nights following Bank Holiday.
Annual Holidays: Last two weeks in January and
first week in July.

How to find:
Campagne is located just under the cities old railway arches, in an area called John's green, the restaurant is in close proximity to Mc Donagh Junction shopping centre.

GPS coordinates
52°8304;39'21" N
7°8304;14'47" W

CARRIG COUNTRY HOUSE

Hidden away on the shores of Caragh Lake, Ring of Kerry, enchanting 'Carrig' offers an 'escape from it all' and the most beautiful scenery in Ireland.

Enjoy golf, fishing, horse riding or hiking. Tour the Ring of Kerry, Dingle Peninsula, Killarney National Park or World Heritage Site Skellig Michael.

Snuggle up in a comfy king size bed and awake to the sound of the lake lapping on the shore. Stroll the wonderful gardens (950 species) or indulge in a good book or game of chess in the spacious Drawing Rooms.

Savour fine wines and mouth-watering Irish Country House cooking in our award winning Lakeside Restaurant.

Frank, Mary and Team extend a warm welcome and unique Irish Country House experience.

Georgina Campbell's Ireland Guide: 'Country House of the Year' 2013.

Bedrooms **17**   Suites **2**   Country House ★ ★ ★ ★

**Carrig Country House & Restaurant,
Caragh Lake, Killorglin, Co.Kerry**
T +353 (0)66 976 9100
info@carrighouse.com www.carrighouse.com

Hosts / Proprietors: Frank & Mary Slattery
Closed December – February inclusive.
Bed & Breakfast per person sharing:
€75 – €145 pps Low Season.
€90 – €175 pps High Season.
Single Supplement: €50.
2 & 3 Day Value Package price on
www.carrighouse.com
Dinner: from €48.50 per person from 7 – 9pm.
A La Carte also available.
Visa, Mastercard, Maestro Accepted.
Children over the age of 8 years are welcome.

How to find:
From Killorglin (10 minutes) – N70 from Killorglin towards Glenbeigh for 4km. After PROMED offices, take 2nd left for Caragh Lake (signposted). At Caragh Lake School and Shop see signpost for Carrig, take sharp right, located 1km further on the left.
From Glenbeigh (10 minutes) – Take the N70 in the direction of Killorglin for 4km, go over one-way stone bridge turning right, continue for approx. 1km and turn right onto the Caragh Lake road (Carrig signpost, before the Red Fox Inn) and drive for 2km. Carrig Country House is on the right.

GPS coordinates
N 52 4' 26.23"
W 9 51' 0.58"

COUNTRY HOUSE & RESTAURANT **CASHEL HOUSE HOTEL**

A perfect romantic hideaway – Cashel House formerly one of Connemara's most gracious homes, set in 50 acres of magnificent gardens on the beautiful coastline of Cashel Bay with Cashel Hill rising behind.

Owned by the McEvilly Family for 50 years, where a warm welcome awaits you. Relax in our Drawing Rooms with its open log fires, antiques and fine arts. Retire to comfortable bedrooms all individually decorated or dine in our restaurant overlooking the garden which serves the finest seafood and meat dishes with vegetables from our garden and region.

Enjoy walking, beaches, sea and lake fishing, golf, horse riding, Connemara ponies in our stud farm, hiking, visit Kylemore Gardens, travel to Aran and Inish Boffin islands or take a boat trip off Killary Fjord.

Bedrooms **17**   Suites **13**   Hotel ★ ★ ★ ★

Cashel House Hotel, Cashel, Co.Galway
T +353 (0)95 31001
F +353 (0)95 31077
res@cashel-house-hotel.com
www.cashel-house-hotel.com

How to find:
South off N59 (Galway Clifden Road).
1.6 kilometres (1 mile) west of Recess, turn left.

Proprietors: The McEvilly Family
Closed January and reopen on 11 February.
Bed and Breakfast €75 – €165 (Low Season)
€80 – €190 (High Season).
Children welcome.
Special Break Rates on request.
Dinner from €32 – €58, also À la Carte.
All major credit cards accepted.
Dog friendly.

CASTLE DURROW

COUNTRY HOUSE & RESTAURANT

Built by Viscount Ashbrook in 1716, in the picturesque village of Durrow, Co.Laois conveniently located about 1 hour from Dublin and 1.5 hours from Cork. Lovingly restored and family home to Peter and Shelly Stokes, Castle Durrow is now one of Ireland's magnificent luxury four star hotels and proudly one of Ireland's most popular wedding venues.

Explore the estate, the surrounding woodlands and river pathways or stroll through our amazing gardens where lots of our organic kitchen produce is grown. Visit the Cafes, Bars, Restaurants and Shops of Durrow, the nearby Heritage Town of Abbeyleix and surrounding historic sites at Kilkenny Castle and Rock of Cashel both 30 mins.

Tripadvisor "Travellers Choice Awards" 2014 – Top 16 in Ireland
Irish Restaurant Awards Winner - 2010 - 2011- 2012 - 2013 and 2014
One Fab Day – Top 100 Wedding Venues 2014

Bedrooms **46 and quirky Gate Lodge**

Castle Durrow, Durrow, Co.Laois
T +353 (0)57 873 6555
F +353 (0)57 873 6559
info@castledurrow.com
www.castledurrow.com
www.facebook.com/CastleDurrow

Proprietors: The Stokes Family
Open all year but closed for Christmas
24–26 December inc
Restaurant Open Wednesday – Sunday
Dinner, Bed & Breakfast from €195 - €250 per couple
Four Course Dinner from €37.50 per person
Sunday Lunch from €27.50 per person
Private Dining Rooms available for special occasions

How to find:
From Dublin: On M7 take exit 17 then N77 through Abbeyleix to Durrow.
From Cork: On M8 take exit 4 then R639 through Johnstown, Cullohill to Durrow.

GPS Coordinates:
Lat: 52.846301
Long: -7.401223

CASTLE LESLIE ESTATE

Steeped in history, full of character and charm, Castle Leslie Estate is the ultimate Irish rural escape. Nestled on 1,000 acres of undulating Irish countryside, dotted with ancient woodland and glittering lakes. Castle Leslie Estate, is one of the last great Irish castle estates still in the hands of its founding family.

The Castle, at the heart of the Estate, offers authentic original interiors and old-style hospitality. Explore the Estate on horseback, enjoy some of Ireland's finest coarse fishing, luxuriate in a relaxing massage or just a stroll through the woods – just some of the choices that await you in this hidden corner of Ireland.

Bedrooms **20**

Specialist accommodation **Historic Castle**

Castle Leslie Estate, Glaslough, Co.Monaghan
T +353 (0)47 88100
info@castleleslie.com
www.castleleslie.com

Proprietor: Sammy Leslie
General Manager: Brian Baldwin
From €140 pps dinner, bed and breakfast.
Single occupancy from €210 dinner,
bed and breakfast.

How to find:
From Dublin take M1 north. Exit at Junction 14 for Ardee. Follow N2 Monaghan/Derry. Continue on the N2 to Monaghan bypass – do not enter town. 1st roundabout follow N2 for Derry. Continue to 3rd roundabout. Take 3rd exit signposted Armagh (N12). Follow N12 for 2 miles. Turn left at signpost for Glaslough (R185). Follow road to Glaslough. 80 minutes from Dublin, 60 minutes from Belfast.

GPS coordinates
Lat: 54.31821
Long: -6.89582

Garmin Loc8 code
G6E-22-5TK

CHAPTER ONE RESTAURANT

Chapter One Restaurant is located in Dublin city centre on the north side of Parnell Square. As a former home of John Jameson, it retains authentic granite walls and sash windows and has been carefully and stylishly renovated to create a wonderfully sumptuous and comfortable restaurant.

It is one of Dublin's leading restaurants having won numerous awards for both food and service. The front of house team are warm and friendly while retaining a high level of efficiency and professionalism.

It is Dublin's premier pre-theatre dining venue. Ross Lewis and Martin Corbett, Chapter One's co-proprietors, have continued to strive for excellence and this effort is manifest throughout the restaurant. A rare treat awaits you.

Chapter One Restaurant
18/19 Parnell Square, Dublin
T +353 (0)1 873 2266
F +353 (0)1 873 2330
info@chapteronerestaurant.com
www.chapteronerestaurant.com

How to find:
Centre of Dublin – Parnell Square
is at the top of O'Connell Street.

Proprietors: Ross Lewis and Martin Corbett
Opening hours:
Lunch: Tuesday – Friday 12.30 – 2.00.
Dinner: Tuesday – Saturday 5.30 – 10.00.
Annual Holidays: Christmas – two weeks;
August – two weeks.
Private Dining: The Jameson Room: 14 people.
The Vault Room: 16 people.

CLARE ISLAND LIGHTHOUSE

The 200 year old Lighthouse, situated on Clare Island in Clew Bay Co. Mayo, has been completely restored and opened for guests in 2013. Its location high on the cliffs, 120 meters above the sea, enables a spectacular vista over the Atlantic Ocean and surrounding areas.

Our interiors, in keeping with the ethos of the Lighthouse, are understated but exceedingly comfortable.

For our guests we prepare fine food, supplemented by local produce, bursting with freshness and flavours complimented by a good selection of International wines.

Accommodation **5 bedrooms/Suites**   Specialist accommodation **Lighthouse**

Clare Island Lighthouse
T +353 (0)87 668 9758
info@clareislandlighthouse.com
www.clareislandlighthouse.com

Proprietor: The Fischer Family
General Manager: Ms Roie Mc Cann
April - October
Special Events November – March
Not suitable for children under 16
Minimum 2 night stay
€350 – €490 pps for 2 nights
includes BB and 6 course Dinner
Single supplement €100
Private dining on request
Dogs by arrangement
Visa and MasterCard accepted.

How to find:
Directions from Westport to Clare Island –
Take the R335 to Louisburgh (20km).
Approximately 1.5km after Louisburgh town take
a right turn for Roonagh Pier (approx 7km).
The ferry sails from Roonagh Pier to Clare Island.
(20 minutes approx.).

GPS coordinates
53.82822 N
-9.98340 E

COOPERSHILL HOUSE

If you are looking for a genuine, romantic, Grand Irish Country House with comfort, character and sublime cooking, then you are going to love Coopershill in Co.Sligo.

A stunning mile long avenue crossing the River Unshin and winding through ancient woods and deer pastures on the 500 acre Private Estate brings you to this fabulous Georgian mansion. Coopershill has been the family home to eight generations of O'Haras and personal attention from the owners is guaranteed.

Perfect for couples on a romantic break or rent the whole house fully catered with family and friends for an unforgettable Private House Party.

Great Taste Awards 2014 2 Gold Stars
Bridgestone Guide 2014 100 Best Places to Stay
Andrew Harper 2013 for Hospitality

Bedrooms **8**   Specialist accommodation **Historic House**

Coopershill House, Riverstown, Co.Sligo
T +353 (0)71 916 5108
ohara@coopershill.com
www.coopershill.com

Proprietor: The O'Hara Family
Open 1 April to end of October.
Open all year for house parties.
Bed & Breakfast:
from €99 – €109 pps low season.
from €109 – €122 pps high season.
Single supplement €35.
4 course dinner at 8.00pm €54.
Dogs and horses by arrangement.

How to find:
On N4 route to Dublin 19km south-east of Sligo. At Drumfin cross roads follow signs to Riverstown and Coopershill.

GPS coordinates
N 54.1381
W 8.4154

CURRAREVAGH HOUSE

Old fashioned (in the best sense of the word), Currarevagh is situated on the shores of Lough Corrib in 150 acres of private woodland estate, now a European Special Area of Conservation. It is run as a private country house rather than an hotel, and the tranquil informality lends itself to those seeking to escape today's hectic world.

Built by the present owner's ancestors in 1842, the exceptional food, cooked by Lucy with flair, originality and passion, and magical grounds take centre stage. Having Connemara and the Aran Islands within easy touring reach, our own boats for guest's use, many walks and abundant wildlife – it all makes a unique, original and wonderful experience not to be missed.

Recent accolades:

Tripadvisor Traveller's Choice 2014 Top 25 Small Hotels in Ireland
Tripadvisor Traveller's Choice 2013 Top 25 Small Hotels in Ireland
Good Hotel Guide Gold Award 2013

Bedrooms **12**   Guesthouse ★ ★ ★ ★

Currarevagh House, Oughterard, Connemara, Co.Galway
T +353 (0)91 552312
 +353 (0)91 552313
F +353 (0)91 552731
rooms@currarevagh.com
www.currarevagh.com

Proprietors: The Hodgson Family
Open 27 March to 31 October
Bed and Breakfast from €70.00 – €90.00 pps
Single Rooms available
Dinner €48.00

How to find:
Take the N59 (Galway/ Clifden) road to Oughterard. Turn right in village square and follow the Glann road for 4 miles (6km).

Extra information:
Reduced Half Board Rates for visits of 2 or more days. Weekly half board rate €795 pp per week. Out of season house parties are welcome (excluding Christmas and New Year).

GPS coordinates
N 53 27.657
W 9 21.518

DUNBRODY HOUSE

COUNTRY HOUSE HOTEL & SPA

Indulgence is the order of the day at Dunbrody with world-renowned gourmet restaurant, chic champagne seafood bar and breakfast 'til Noon daily. Couple this foodie focus with our aim to please and pamper and you get a feel for what Dunbrody House is loved for. Set in 300 acres of parkland on the idyllic Hook Peninsula on Ireland's south coast, 1830s Dunbrody really is the perfect year-round choice for a romantic getaway to the country.

For the culinary inquisitives there's the temptation of our cookery school with a range of 1 & 2 day and weeklong courses with Julien, our very qualified chef/ instructor.

Luxury treatments in our boutique spa are hard to resist too.

"Ease, elegance, excellence" Seamus Heaney, Poet Laureate

Bedrooms **22** including Suites and Guest Lodge   Hotel ★ ★ ★ ★

**Dunbrody Country House Hotel,
Arthurstown, Co.Wexford**
T +353 (0)51 389600
F +353 (0)51 389601
info@dunbrodyhouse.com
www.dunbrodyhouse.com

Proprietors: Catherine & Kevin Dundon
B&B from €75 – €155 pps low season,
€95 – €195 pps high season.
Single Supplement €25 per night on
standard double rooms.
Seasonal 5 course Dinner Menu €55 – €65 and
€80 8 course Tasting Menu.

How to find:
M11/N11 from south Dublin and then the
R733 to Arthurstown.
M9 from north Dublin to New Ross and then the
R733 to Arthurstown.
N25 from Cork/Waterford and the Passage East
car ferry to Ballyhack / Arthurstown.
Aer Lingus and FlyBe from London,
Birmingham and Manchester to
Waterford.

ENNISCOE HOUSE

Hidden among the woods at the foot of Nephin is Enniscoe, 'the last Great House of North Mayo' overlooking the waters of Lough Conn. The estate has been in the family since the 1650s and the classical Georgian house dates from the 1790s.

The current generation, Susan Kellett and her son Dj, are happy to share their house and grounds with guests. There are elegant reception rooms and fine bedrooms with stunning views over lake and park. Outside are pastures, shrubberies, miles of woodland and lakeside walks, a carefully restored Victorian pleasure garden and an organic vegetable garden. Good food, freshly prepared, uses fruit and vegetables from the garden as well as other local produce.

Bedrooms **6**

Specialist accommodation **Historic House**

Enniscoe House, Castlehill, Ballina, Co.Mayo
T +353 (0)96 31112
F +353 (0)96 31773
mail@enniscoe.com
www.enniscoe.com

Proprietor: Susan Kellett and Dj Kellett
Open 1 April to 31 October.
Open all year for house parties.
Bed & Breakfast from €80 – €120 pps.
Dinner €50 at 7.30 – 8.00pm.
Single supplement €20.
Dogs welcome.

How to find:
Enniscoe is 3.2km south of the village of Crossmolina on the R315 to Pontoon and Castlebar. It is 20km from Ballina.

GPS coordinates
N 54.075060
W -9.312633

GHAN HOUSE

Built in 1727, Ghan House is a listed Georgian House set within 3 acres of walled gardens.

Located a tree length from medieval Carlingford, with its' narrow streets, town gate, castles, priory & ancient walls. Ghan House is just one hour from both Dublin and Belfast.

The 2 AA Rosette awarded restaurant utilises the herb & vegetable gardens and celebrates the house's position on Carlingford Lough with the local seafood and Cooley mountain lamb and beef.

Whether you stay in the old house or one of the garden bedrooms views of Carlingford Lough, the Mourne mountains or Slieve Foy come as standard.

John & Sally McKenna's "Best 100 Places to stay in Ireland" every year since 1999

"Best 100 Wedding Venues in Ireland 2013 & 2014" **One Fab Day**

Bedrooms **12**   Specialist accommodation **Historic House**

Ghan House, Carlingford, Co.Louth
T +353 (0)42 937 3682
info@ghanhouse.com
www.ghanhouse.com

Proprietor: Paul & Joyce Carroll
Open all year.
(Closed 24 – 26th, 31st December & 1st & 2nd January)
B&B from €75 pps – €125 pps
Single bedroom available, no supplement.
4 course dinner €47.50, most nights
6pm – 9.30pm
6 course midweek tasting menu €36.50
6pm to 7.45pm
Special midweek & weekend dinner & B&B breaks.

All major credit cards accepted.
No service charge. Gratuities at discretion of guests.

How to find:
Take junction 18 on main Dublin to Belfast M1 to Carlingford. On the left, 10 metres after 50kph sign on entrance to Carlingford is a stone entrance & gravel drive to Ghan House.

GPS coordinates
N54°02.373' W006°11.044' /
54.04028, - 6.18417

GREGANS CASTLE

With breathtaking views across Galway Bay and idyllically situated overlooking the unique Burren landscape, this is the ultimate luxury and gourmet hideaway.

Simon and Frederieke manage this oasis of comfort and offer genuine Irish hospitality, award winning innovative cooking and elegant bedrooms free from the intrusion of televisions. Antiques, modern art, turf fires, candlelight and garden flowers add to the indulgently relaxing atmosphere.

The ideal location from which to enjoy the Burren, Cliffs of Moher, Walking, Cycling, the Aran Islands, Horse Riding, Surfing, Sea Angling and Golf.

Awards include:
Food & Wine Magazine Best Restaurant & Best Chef Munster 2014,
RAI Best Hotel Restaurant 2014, **AA** 3 Rosettes 2014; **Gold Medal Awards** Best Country House 2013, **AA** Hotel of the Year 2012, **NHA** Best Hotel Restaurant 2012, **Food & Wine Magazine** Best Restaurant & Best Chef 2011
Recommended by **Andrew Harper** and **Alastair Sawday's**

Bedrooms **15**   Suites **6**   Hotel ★ ★ ★ ★

Gregans Castle Hotel,
The Burren, Ballyvaughan, Co.Clare
T +353 (0)65 7077005
stay@gregans.ie
www.gregans.ie

Proprietors: Simon Haden and
Frederieke McMurray
General Manager: Ken Bergin
Bed & Breakfast: €112.50 to €132.50pps.
Supplement for Superior Rooms and Suites.
Single Supplement from €60.00 to €65.00.
Dinner from €55.00 to €75.00.
Open from February 13th to November 7th.

How to find:
On N67, 5km south of Ballyvaughan village.
Only 1 hour from Shannon Airport and 2½ hours from Dublin.

GPS coordinates
53 04 36 79 N
9 11 11 19 W

HAYFIELD MANOR

Nestled within walled gardens, Cork's premier 5 star hotel, Hayfield Manor provides the charm of a country house with vibrant Cork city on the doorstep. Boasting a choice of splendid accommodation, rooms and suites are classically styled. Guests with a penchant for exquisite food will enjoy Orchids Gourmet Restaurant and Perrotts Garden Bistro.

Traditional Afternoon Tea is served in luxuriously appointed reception areas, including The Manor Bar, Drawing Room, Library and enclosed gardens. The Beautique Spa features Elemis Spa Therapy, an indoor heated pool, Jacuzzi, steam room and resident's gym. Our concierge is on hand to assist you discover the unique attractions of Cork city and county.

Bedrooms **88**   Suites **4**   Hotel ★ ★ ★ ★ ★

Hayfield Manor, Perrott Avenue, College Road, Cork
T +353 (0)21 484 5900
F +353 (0)21 431 6839
enquiries@hayfieldmanor.ie
www.hayfieldmanor.ie

Proprietors: Joe and Margaret Scally
Managers: Anne-Marie Scally and Ettienne Van Vrede
Open all year round.
Manor Rooms: €89 pps to €190 pps.
Superior and Junior Suites also available.
Suites: €245 pps to €515 pps.
Perrotts Garden Bistro: A la Carte.
Orchids: 5 course Gourmet Menu – €65 per person.

Afternoon Tea: 1.30pm – 4.30pm.
Private dining available.
Service charge of 10% on 8 people or more.
All major credit cards accepted.
Wheelchair accessible rooms available.

How to find:
6 Miles from Cork International Airport (ORK) 80 Miles from Shannon International Airport (SNN). Hayfield Manor, located off College Road opposite UCC.

GPS coordinates
N 51.89102
W -8.48953

HUNTER'S HOTEL

Ireland's oldest coaching inn, in the 5th generation of the same family. Its picturesque gardens along the banks of the river Vartry provide a delightful setting for a delicious lunch, afternoon tea or a drink.

An ideal base from which to visit Mount Usher Gardens, Powerscourt, Russborough, Killruddery and Glendalough in County Wicklow, 'The Garden of Ireland'.

There are fifteen 18-hole golf courses nearby, most notably Druid's Glen and the European. Horse riding and hill walking can be arranged. Conference facilities available. Hunter's is approx. 60 minutes drive from Dublin, 30 minutes from Dun Laoghaire and 90 minutes from Rosslare.

Bedrooms **16**   Specialist accommodation **Hotel & Restaurant**

Hunter's Hotel, Newrath Bridge, Rathnew, Co.Wicklow
T +353 (0)404 40106
F +353 (0)404 40338
reception@hunters.ie
www.hunters.ie

Proprietor: Gelletlie Family
Closed 24, 25, 26 & 31 December.
Bed & Breakfast from €65 – €95 per person.
Dinner from €29.50 served 7.30pm to 8.45pm.
Lunch from €18.75 served 1.00pm to 2.40pm.
Afternoon Tea €12.00 served from 4.00pm.
Private dining available.
No Service Charge.

How to find:
From Dublin: Take exit 15 for Ashford off the N11.
Turn left at the bridge in Ashford. Then 2km.
From Wexford/Rosslare: Take exit 16 for Ashford off the N11. Pass Mount Usher Gardens.
Turn right at bridge in Ashford. Then 2km.

GPS coordinates
N 53.006374
W -6.084328

ICE HOUSE

The Ice House, perched on the banks of the majestic River Moy, is a stunning fusion of traditional and modern, with a history dating back to the mid-19th century, featuring a mix of heritage and contemporary accommodation, all with panoramic river views.

Chef Anthony Holland works with the finest seasonal local produce in the Restaurant.

Chill Spa is a VOYA exclusive spa, with 5 luxurious treatment rooms, a spa thermal suite and an outdoor spa garden featuring riverside hot tubs and a cedar barrel sauna.

Nearby activities include golf (Enniscrone, Carne and Rosses Point a short drive), horse riding or fishing on the Moy.

Awards:
Tatler Spa Awards – Best Boutique Spa 2014 & Best Spa Therapist 2014
Golfers Guide to Ireland – Best Boutique Hotel 2014

Bedrooms / Suites **32**   Hotel ★ ★ ★ ★

The Ice House, The Quay, Ballina, Co.Mayo
T +353 (0)96 23500
chill@theicehouse.ie
www.theicehouse.ie

Proprietor: Pearse Farrell
Open all year round.
Closed 24 – 26 December.
Deluxe Rooms from €69 pps B&B,
Suites from €89 pps B&B.
Single Occupancy supplement €50.
Dinner: €45.
Children welcome.

How to find:
From Dublin – Follow N4/M4 route direction Sligo. At Longford follow N5 route direction Westport. Turn right onto N26 outside Swinford direction Foxford and Ballina. On arrival in Ballina, follow N59 direction Sligo through the town and across the river. Turn left at traffic lights onto Quay Road. The Ice House is located ca. 1km on The Quay.

Celebrating 40 years, Aidan and Joan MacManus have earned an international reputation for fresh seafood and hospitality in their harbourside restaurant in the picturesque fishing village of Howth. Panoramic sea views, the lapping of the water, the sounds of the sea birds … only 20 minutes from Dublin Airport and 25 minutes by DART into Dublin.

Chef Patron Aidan cooks fresh fish landed daily on the Pier, with Lobster caught by our own fishermen a particular favourite. Now with East Cafe Bar open all day for casual dining and socialising. Howth at leisure – walking, sailing and golf. Lots to do – stay a few days!

Bedrooms **8**   Guesthouse ★ ★ ★ ★

King Sitric, Fish Restaurant & Accommodation, East Pier, Howth, Co.Dublin
T +353 (0)1 832 5235, F +353 (0)1 839 2442
info@kingsitric.ie
www.kingsitric.ie

Proprietors: The MacManus Family
Bed & Breakfast from €65 pps.
Special short breaks available.
Babies and children welcome – under 12s sharing with parents free.
Small dogs by arrangement.
Dinner Wednesday – Saturday from 6.30pm.
Sundays 1.00pm – 5.00pm.
East Cafe Bar open from 10.30am all day.
Check for winter hours.
Private Dining, Weddings, Meetings, etc.

How to find:
Coming in to Howth, all the way across the harbour front to the end of the road, top of the far pier.

GPS coordinates
Latitude 53.23 18 N
Longitude 06.03 48 W

Established in 1989 and located on Lower Baggot Street in the heart of Georgian Dublin, Michelin Star l'Ecrivain is a modern, contemporary restaurant. Run by Chef Derry Clarke and his wife Sallyanne, this award-winning restaurant has a reputation for innovative cooking Irish/French style using the very best of Irish produce from small indigenous producers all in season.

l'Ecrivain has two private dining rooms, the Malt room on the ground floor seats 12 people and the Salon Privè seats 18 people. Derry Clarke is renowned for his culinary expertise, and together with his team of chefs, Sallyanne and the front of house team, l'Ecrivain is an experience not to be missed.

l'Ecrivain Restaurant
109a Lower Baggot Street, Dublin 2
T +353 (0)1 661 1919
F +353 (0)1 661 0617
enquiries@lecrivain.com
www.lecrivain.com

Proprietors: Derry and Sallyanne Clarke
Extensive Wine List and Cocktail List available.
Main Restaurant seats 90.
The Malt Room – Private Dining Room seats 12.
Salon Privè – Private Dining Room seats 18.
Lunch from €25.
Dinner: 2 Course €60, 3 Course €75.
Lunch: Thursday and Friday 12.30pm to 2.00pm.
Dinner: Monday to Saturday 6.30pm to 10.30pm.
Reservations recommended.

LISS ARD ESTATE

The 100 acre estate is a place for relaxation, offering a variety of accommodation in a seamless blend of contemporary styles in the surrounds of the old world charm in the 19th century Country House, the adjacent Garden Mews and the Lake Lodge.

The enthusiastic culinary team in the newly designed 'Restaurant at Liss Ard' serves food that is fresh, clean & crisp, complimenting local producers with in-house creations.

It is a magical place for those seeking a little time out, solitude and peace to reflect while experiencing the unique James Turrell Crater, exploring the woods, immersing in the simplicity of yoga or spending time on Lake Abisdealy.

Sunday Business Post – *"Liss Ard walks a fine line between classical and modern luxury, and does it well. We'll be back!"*

Bedrooms **25**

Specialist accommodation **Historic House**

Liss Ard Estate, Castletownsend Road, Skibbereen, Co.Cork
T:+353 (0)28 40000
F:+353 (0)28 40001
reservations@lissardestate.com
www.lissardestate.com

Proprietor: The Stern Family
Rooms from €150 – €450
The 'Restaurant at Liss Ard' seats up to 100 guests, open Wednesday – Sunday, reservations highly recommended, à-la-carte Dinner, 3 courses, from €35
Pet friendly rooms available, dogs are very welcome
Trip Advisor 2014 Winner

How to find:
Liss Ard is two minutes from Skibbereen town centre. From Cork Airport, follow the N71 to West Cork & Skibbereen. At Skibbereen follow the one way system to the Regal Roundabout with the LIDL Retail Shop. Take the first exit and follow the signs to Castletownsend, A596. The entrance to the Liss Ard Estate is less than 1 kilometre on the right-hand-side.

GPS coordinates
51.532348250305326 (Latitude)
-9.249801635742188 (Longitude)

LONGUEVILLE HOUSE
COUNTRY HOUSE & RESTAURANT

Set in 500 acres of wooded estate in North Co Cork, Longueville House (c1720) is a romantic Georgian Heritage Mansion owned and run by the O'Callaghan family. An ideal venue for residential wedding parties (130 Guests), meetings and group get togethers. Longueville offers on-site salmon & brown trout fishing on the River Blackwater, Simulated Clay Shooting, May dawn chorus Walks & Autumn Mushroom Hunts. A Walled Kitchen Garden & Working Farm, Brandy Distillery & Cider House all to explore on-site! At the heart of Longueville is The Presidents' Restaurant, with a field to fork policy offering the freshest produce from our gardens & farm with kitchen supervised by internationally commended chef/patron William O'Callaghan.

Awards include:

One Fab Day 100 Best Wedding Venues 2014, 2013
Georgina Campbell Natural Food Awards 2014
Irish Food Awards 2013 for Apple Brandy - Spirits Section
Cider Ireland Taste & Presentation – Best in Class 2013
Euro Toques Food Award for Cider 2013

Bedrooms **14**   Junior Suites **6**   Listed Heritage Property ★ ★ ★ ★

Longueville House and Presidents' Restaurant, Mallow, Co.Cork
T +353 (0)22 47156
F +353 (0)22 47459
info@longuevillehouse.ie
www.longuevillehouse.ie

Proprietor: The O'Callaghan Family
Rates: Bed & Breakfast €90 – €130 pps. Single supplements apply. Dinner menu from €49, served 6.30 – 9.00pm. Opens Wednesday to Sunday inclusive year round. Opens for groups 20 Guests + Mon/Tues by prior arrangement. Winter opening hours more limited, consult hotel website.

How to find:
3 miles west of Mallow via the N72 road to Killarney. Take the second Ballyclough junction on the right hand side (approx. 3 miles from Mallow roundabout) and hotel entrance is 100 yards on left-hand side where a welcome awaits.

GPS coordinates
N52° 08. 308
W008° 44.188

MARLFIELD HOUSE

Marlfield is a beautifully restored charming Regency period house set on 36 acres of gardens and filled with gleaming antiques and paintings. It is situated outside Gorey, well known for its boutiques and one hour from Dublin. Its elegant and luxurious bedrooms overlook the extensive grounds and the renowned conservatory dining room with frescoed walls is highly acclaimed using home grown and local produce. Delicious food, luxurious surroundings and impeccable service provide the romantic and ultimate escape from it all.

Opening in 2015 the courtyard has been converted into a casual dining option with the addition of a bistro serving simple fresh food. Marlfield hosts exclusive use house wedding parties and from 2015 will also cater for 'barn weddings' in the courtyard.

2014 Winner of the **Restaurant Association of Ireland** Best Customer Service Award in Leinster.

Bedrooms **13**   State Rooms **6**

Marlfield House, Courtown Road R742, Gorey, Co.Wexford
T +353 (0)53 94 21124
F +353 (0)53 94 21572
info@marlfieldhouse.ie
www.marlfieldhouse.com
Proprietor: The Bowe Family
General Managers: Margaret and Laura Bowe
Open 1 March to 2 January, open all year for weddings and special events.
B&B: Bedrooms from €80 – €125 pps.
State Bedrooms: €120 – €310 pps.
Single room from €80.
Supper Menu from €36, Sunday lunch €45, Five course dinner €65, Lunch in the garden or Library, Monday to Saturday from €25.

How to find:
Marlfield is 75km south of Dublin off the N11 and is located just outside the town of Gorey on the Courtown Road R742. From Exit 23 on the N11 follow signs for Courtown, at Courtown Road roundabout turn left for Gorey. The hotel is less than a mile on the left hand side. From Gorey follow signs for Courtown R742, hotel is less than one mile from the town on the right.

GPS coordinates
N 52 40 06
W 06 16 46

THE MERRION HOTEL

The Merrion, Dublin's most stylish 5 star hotel is situated opposite Government Buildings in the city centre. Created from four Georgian Townhouses and a contemporary Garden Wing, the 142 bedrooms and suites are arranged around beautifully manicured gardens. Stunningly restored interiors provide the backdrop for one of Ireland's most impressive art collections.

Guests have the choice of two bars and two restaurants, including the 2 Michelin - starred Restaurant Patrick Guilbaud and The Cellar Restaurant.

Additional features include Georgian Drawing Rooms where Art Afternoon Tea is served daily, and The Tethra Spa which boasts an 18m pool, gymnasium, steam room and treatment rooms.

Recent Awards: **World's Best Places to Stay** – Conde Nast Traveler – 2014
Best Hotel Restaurant – The Cellar Restaurant, Restaurant Association of Ireland – 2014
Top 500 World's Best Hotels – Travel & Leisure – 2013
World's Best Service – Ranked in the 'Top 10' in the world for service, Travel & Leisure - 2011

Bedrooms **123**   Suites **19**   Hotel ★ ★ ★ ★ ★

The Merrion Hotel,
Upper Merrion Street, Dublin 2
T +353 (0)1 603 0600
F +353 (0)1 603 0700
info@merrionhotel.com
www.merrionhotel.com

General Manager: Peter MacCann
Published Rates:
From €480 – €3,000 per room, per night.

GDS Code: LW8430.

How to find:
Located in Dublin city centre on Upper Merrion Street, opposite Government Buildings.

GPS coordinates
Lat: 53.338596
Long: -6.252956

LUXURY COUNTRY HOUSE & ESTATE

MOUNT JULIET
HOTEL & ESTATE

Steeped in heritage, Mount Juliet is one of Ireland's leading country estates, famed for the welcome and exceptional service.

Experience everything Mount Juliet has to offer including dinner in the 1 Michelin Star Lady Helen restaurant, golf on the Jack Nicklaus course, a luxury spa treatment, river & lake fishing, equestrian centre with extensive trails, woodland walks and much more.

Mount Juliet is a wonderfully relaxed location for a luxury break in the South East; located 20 minutes from the medieval city of Kilkenny & just over 1 hour from Dublin.

Awards 2014
Hotel – AA 4 Red Stars & Tripadvisor Travellers' Choice Top 25 Luxury Hotels in Ireland
The Lady Helen Restaurant - 3 AA Rosettes & the Best Hotel Restaurant at the Irish Restaurant Awards

---

Bedrooms **31**   Luxury Country House & Estate ★ ★ ★ ★

**Mount Juliet Country Estate,
Thomastown, Co.Kilkenny**
T +353 (0)56 777 3000
info@mountjuliet.ie
www.mountjuliet.ie

General Manager: Mr. William Kirby
Open all year round.
B&B Low Season:
€139 – €279 per room per night.
B&B High Season:
€169 – €369 per room per night.

How to find:
From Dublin: Take the N7/M7 (Naas Road) – branch onto the M9, signposted 'Waterford, Carlow & Kilkenny' which is Exit 11 on the M7. Follow the M9 and take Exit 9 signposted 'Kilkenny/Stoneyford'. At the top of the ramp turn left onto the N10 heading for Stoneyford. Drive straight through the village of Stoneyford and at the end of the village at the fork in the road (at the school) take the left hand turn, signposted 'Mount Juliet 4km'. After 4km, Mount Juliet will be on the left.

GPS Coordinates:
N 52° 31' 33.00"
W 07° 11' 13.00"

With breath-taking views overlooking the Atlantic Ocean, Moy House is a beautifully restored early 19th century home set on 15 acres.

A romantic 'home away from home' where a contemporary and elegant ambience is combined with warm hospitality. Nine beautifully restored individually designed bedrooms. Dinner can be enjoyed in the conservatory restaurant as the sun sets over the Atlantic.

Located minutes from world famous championships links golf courses, Moy House is a haven for the keen golfer.

Intimate venue for small weddings.

Awards include:
2 **AA** Rosettes for Culinary Excellence
Food & Wine Magazine: 'Style Award' 2012
Georgina Campbell's: 'Hideaway of the Year' 2013

Bedrooms **9**   Suites **1**   Guesthouse ★ ★ ★ ★

Moy House, Lahinch, Co.Clare
T +353 (0)65 708 2800
moyhouse@eircom.net
www.moyhouse.com

Proprietor: Antoin O'Looney
Closed November – March.
Bed and Breakfast from €92.50 – €140 pps.
Luxury Suites from €135 – €180 pps.
Special packages also available.
Gourmet Tasting Menu €60.

How to find:
Moy House is located 1km outside Lahinch on N67 Miltown Malbay Road.

Shannon airport 50km
Lahinch Golf Course 2km
Doonbeg Golf Course 28km

GPS coordinates
Lat: 52.951381
Long: -9.346285

THE MUSTARD SEED

Nestled in the heart of the countryside, The Mustard Seed sits on seven colourful acres overlooking the rustic village of Ballingarry. Just down the road from Adare, the restaurant is legendary with orchard and herb gardens providing synergy with the kitchen. A heritage hideaway, the perfect venue for exclusive weddings, civil ceremonies and family gatherings.

Located 40 minutes from Shannon airport, this stylish home is an ideal base for touring the south west region. Close to the Ballyhoura Mountain range. Resident Thai masseur by appointment.

Recent awards include:
'Best Customer Service' 2014 **Food & Wine Awards.**
'Best Hotel Restaurant' 2014 **National Hospitality Awards.**
'Hideaway of the Year' 2014 **Georgina Campbell.**
'Pet Friendly Hotel of the Year' 2014 **Georgina Campbell.**
'Best Restaurant in Ireland 2013' **The Hotel & Catering Gold Medal Awards.**

Bedrooms **14**   Suites **3**   Hotel ★ ★ ★ ★

The Mustard Seed,
Ballingarry, Co.Limerick
T +353 (0)69 68508
mustard@indigo.ie
www.mustardseed.ie

Proprietor: Daniel Mullane
B&B rates: €70 – €165 pps.
Single supplement: From €15.
Classic House menu: €60.
Early Evening Dinner: €45.
Pets by arrangement.
Children welcome.
Wheelchair friendly.

How to find:
From Limerick: From the top of Adare village, take the N21 Killarney road for half a mile. Turn left at the first road junction to the left and follow the signposts for Ballingarry village.
From Kerry: Travel along the N21. Look for signs for Rathkeale. In Rathkeale town, follow the R518 for four miles to Ballingarry village.

GPS coordinates
Lat: 52.474672
Long: 8.864692

NEWFORGE HOUSE

Cradled in beautiful gardens and green fields, Newforge House offers warm hospitality and superb food in the tranquil surroundings of our Georgian Country House. Our light, airy rooms blend antiques with contemporary comforts and offer uninterrupted views of our gardens and countryside.

Food is central to the Newforge experience. John showcases the best local seasonal produce – some of which comes from our own gardens and orchard – in our daily changing dinner menu. And our friendly hens provide wonderful eggs for Breakfast!

Our central location makes Newforge a perfect base for touring Northern Ireland, with Lough Neagh around the corner and Belfast just 30 minutes drive.

Awards include:
Georgina Campbell's Ireland Guide: 'Country House of the Year' 2014, 'Best Country House Breakfast 2014' & 'Irish Breakfast Awards National Winner 2014'
Good Food Ireland's 'Culinary Haven of the Year' 2014
RAI: 'Best Hotel Restaurant in Ulster' 2014
L&C News: 'Best Guesthouse in Northern Ireland' 2014

Bedrooms **6**   Guesthouse ★ ★ ★ ★ ★

Newforge House, 58 Newforge Road, Magheralin, Co.Armagh, BT67 0QL
T +44 (0)28 926 11255
enquiries@newforgehouse.com
www.newforgehouse.com

Proprietor: John & Louise Mathers
Open: 31 January – 21 December.
Bed & Breakfast £60 – £90 per person sharing.
Single supplement £20 – £25.
Special mid-week, weekend and multiple-night breaks available.
3-Course Dinner £40, served at 8pm,
Tues. – Sat. Available with 24 hour's notice.
Light meal options available on Sunday and Monday evenings.

How to find:
From Belfast: M1 West, exit 9, Moira follow 5km. In Magheralin left at Byrne's pub: left after national speed limit sign.
From Newry: A1 north towards Belfast. Follow c. 30km, exit Dromore onto B2 (Lurgan Road). Continue 8km, take right onto Newforge Road B9. Continue 1km: 200m on right after bridge.

GPS coordinates
N 54.4619 W -6.2577

NEWPORT HOUSE

A Historic Georgian House in gardens and park adjoining the town and overlooking the Newport river and quay. For two hundred years it was the home of the O'Donnells, once the Earls of Tir Connell.

Famous as an angling centre Newport House offers preserved salmon and sea trout fishing on the Newport river (8 miles) and Lough Beltra.

The cuisine is based on fresh local produce and is complemented by an extensive cellar which includes many of the classical vintages. The house is furnished with many fine antiques and paintings which provide an elegant setting for a quiet and relaxing holiday.

Bedrooms **10**   Hotel ★ ★ ★ ★

Newport House, Newport, Co.Mayo
T +353 (0)98 41222
info@newporthouse.ie
www.newporthouse.ie

How to find:
In the town of Newport.

Proprietor: Kieran Thompson
Open 19th March to the end of October.
B&B: from €95.00 – €125.00 Low Season
       from €110.00 – €140.00 High Season.
No Single Supplement.
No Service Charge.
5 Course Dinner €65.00 also à la carte
from 7.00 pm., to last orders 9.00 p.m.

Since 1897 many world travellers have enjoyed the pleasure of the Park Hotel Kenmare and its renowned restaurant. Set in a heavenly location overlooking Kenmare Bay the hotel is in the heart of Ireland's most scenic countryside. All accommodations are spacious with sitting area, antique furnishings and original art while Deluxe and Suites enjoy a full sea view or private veranda.

Home to the Deluxe Destination Spa SÁMAS guests can experience the virtues of a true spa. This special and quite unique place blends healing and therapeutic traditions from the East and West with the life inspiring scenery of Kerry to revive the body, mind and soul.

Sunday Times – 2014 – Top 20 Chefs Favourite Foodie Hotels
Sunday Times – 2013 – Top 10 Hotels in Ireland
Conde Nast Traveler – 2012 – Gold List - Best Hotel in Ireland
Member of **Relais & Chateaux**

Bedrooms **37**   Suites **9**   Hotel ★ ★ ★ ★ ★

Park Hotel Kenmare, Kenmare, Co.Kerry
T +353 (0)64 664 1200
F +353 (0)64 664 1402
info@parkkenmare.com
www.parkkenmare.com

How to find:
'Top of Town'.

Managing Director: John Brennan
Open – April 3rd – October 26th;
December 23rd – January 2nd
Double/Twin €145 – €406 pps B&B.
Dinner €68.
Two Night Packages from €345 pps.
Wheelchair facilities.
Children welcome.

RATHMULLAN HOUSE

With its stunning location, right beside the sea, you can stroll through the gardens of this lovely old house down to a mile long sandy beach. Inside has a comfortable and informal country house style with rooms to suit everyone, from romantic garden rooms to large garret rooms for whole families. An indoor pool and holistic treatments add to the relaxation.

Being beside the sea, fresh fish is guaranteed. Local food and produce from the walled garden supplies the kitchen. Nearby, there are lots of excellent links providing golf at great value.

Check out our website for 1, 2 and 3 day itineraries.

Awards include:
AA 2 Rosettes 2014
One Fab Day 100 Best Wedding Venues 2014
Dalemain Marmalade Award Winner 2014

Bedrooms **32**   Hotel ★ ★ ★ ★

Rathmullan House, Rathmullan, Co.Donegal
T +353 (0)74 915 8188, F +353 (0)74 915 8200
info@rathmullanhouse.com
www.rathmullanhouse.com

Proprietor: The Wheeler Family
Open full time from: March to October,
Winter Weekends, Half Terms & New Year.
B&B from €80 – €115 pps low season.
From €100 – €135 pps high season.
Single rooms available at no supplement.
Children welcome, busy with families
during holiday times.
A la carte supper and dinner available 6pm to 8:45pm
10% Service charge on extras only.

How to find:
From Letterkenny go to Ramelton (R245) and on to
Rathmullan (R247). Turn left at butchers, through
village heading north and gates are on the right.

GPS coordinates
N 55.0989383
W 7.53266

RATHSALLAGH HOUSE COUNTRY HOUSE & RESTAURANT

Converted from Queen Anne stables in 1798, Rathsallagh is a large comfortable house situated in 530 acres of peaceful parkland with a walled garden surrounded by an 18-hole Championship Golf Course. Close to Glendalough, the Wicklow mountains, The National Stud (with its Japanese Gardens) and the Curragh, yet Dublin is less than one hour's drive.

The food is Country house cooking at its best and is organically produced by local growers and in Rathsallagh's gardens. The atmosphere is relaxed with log and turf fires and luxurious bedrooms. Rathsallagh can cater for conferences, meetings and weddings for up to 250 guests.

The O'Flynn family and their staff look forward to welcoming you to Rathsallagh.

Bedrooms **35**

Rathsallagh House, Dunlavin, Co.Wicklow
T +353 (0)45 403112, F +353 (0)45 403343
info@rathsallagh.com
www.rathsallagh.com

How to find:
Signposted from Dunlavin.
Less than 1 hour from Dublin Airport.
15km Naas off the M9.

Proprietor: The O'Flynn Family
Open all year round.
Bed & Breakfast from €190 per room.
Single Supplement from €50.
Dinner from €35.
Golf for residents from €35.
Open for Sunday lunch.
Prior reservation essential.
Available for private fully serviced rentals.

RESTAURANT FORTY ONE

Under the expert guidance of award-winning Chef Graham Neville, Restaurant FortyOne has flourished.

Graham and his team create delicate, elegant dishes, using the finest ingredients from their very own garden in Kenah Hill, Killiney.

Looking over the beauty of Stephen's Green, the dining room of Restaurant FortyOne is an intimate and serene setting in the heart of Dublin city.

The staff, meanwhile, are attentive and mindful. This is fine-dining without the stuffiness.

Recent awards:

2013 & 2014 **Food and Wine Magazine** Best Dublin Restaurant

2013 & 2014 **Food and Wine Magazine** Best Dublin Chef

2014 **Food and Wine Magazine** Chef of the Year

Restaurant Forty One
41 St Stephen's Green, Dublin 2
T +353 (0)1 662 0000
info@restaurantfortyone.ie
www.restaurantfortyone.ie

How to find:
St. Stephen's Green East, opposite the Green

Proprietor: Olivia Gaynor Long
Opening Hours: Tuesday – Saturday
(Lunch: 12.30pm – 2.30pm)
(Dinner: 5.30pm – 10.30pm)
Annual Holidays: First two weeks in August and
after lunch on December 24th – December 31st
for dinner

RESTAURANT PATRICK GUILBAUD

Established in 1981, Restaurant Patrick Guilbaud is Ireland's top restaurant, holder of two Michelin stars as well as virtually all the top national and international awards. It is situated in an 18th century Georgian Townhouse adjoining the Merrion Hotel. It houses an impressive collection of Irish Art.

This bright, elegant restaurant, run by Stephane Robin, serves modern classic cuisine using the best Irish produce in season. Chef Guillaume Lebrun's signature dishes include the Lobster Ravioli, Roast Challans Duck, Assiette Gourmande au Chocolat.

The wine list is very impressive in both its depth and its range – do take time to peruse it.

Covers **85**

Restaurant Patrick Guilbaud,
21 Upper Merrion Street, Dublin 2
T +353 (0)1 6764 192
F +353 (0)1 6610 052
info@restaurantpatrickguilbaud.ie
www.restaurantpatrickguilbaud.ie

Proprietor: Patrick Guilbaud
Chef: Guillaume Lebrun
Manager: Stephane Robin
Open: Tuesday to Saturday.
Closed: 25 December – 7 January.
Lunch: 12.30 – 2.15pm. Dinner: 7.00 – 10.15pm.
Lunch Menu: €40 (2 courses); €50 (3 courses).
Except December.
Special Christmas Lunch Menu €70 for
all December.

Seasonal Tasting Menu: €90 available only from
Tuesday to Friday.
À la carte available for lunch and dinner.
Private Dining Room.

How to find:
Opposite Government buildings.
Merrion Street.

ROSLEAGUE MANOR

A beautifully situated Georgian house overlooking Ballinakill Bay, which has been lovingly converted into a first-class hotel with a Victorian style conservatory and delightful drawing rooms with open log fires. All of the bedrooms are individually decorated and feature fine antiques and paintings.

Set in 30 acres of secluded woodland on the ocean's edge, Rosleague is located just one mile from the Connemara National Park, an area of some 5,000 acres and just 5 minutes drive from Kylemore Abbey and it's beautiful walled gardens.

Cuisine is based on the freshest and finest of ingredients, with local seafood and Connemara lamb a specialty.

Sunday Independent – *"As such, Rosleague Manor's Summer Eden is a hard stage to beat."*

Independent Traveller – *"Rosleague manor is a beautiful & peaceful place... A gem in Connemara"*

Bedrooms **16**   Junior Suites **4**   Listed Heritage Hotel ★ ★ ★ ★

**Rosleague Manor, Letterfrack,
Connemara, Co.Galway**
T +353 (0)95 41101
F +353 (0)95 41168
info@rosleague.com
www.rosleague.com

How to find:
N59, seven miles north
west from Clifden.

GPS coordinates
N 53.5514
W 9.9716

Proprietors: Edmund and Mark Foyle
Open: 15 March – 1 November.
B&B from €70 – €115 pps.
Single supplement €30.
2 Course Dinner €32.
4 Course Dinner €46.
Special short break rates on request.
Dog Friendly.
Exclusive residential wedding parties: 95 max.

STELLA MARIS
COUNTRY HOUSE HOTEL

Located directly on the spectacular Wild Atlantic Way, Stella Maris Country House Hotel was built in 1853 as a regional coastguard headquarters, and later served as a convent. In 2002 Stella Maris Country House Hotel re-opened its doors after an extensive two-year restoration. Guests may enjoy unique views of the Wild Atlantic Way from our 100-foot oceanfront conservatory. Downpatrick Head, one of the Discovery Points of the Wild Atlantic Way, is part of our unique coastal vista.

Proprietor Frances Kelly oversees the kitchen, featuring home-garden organic produce in the menu that changes daily. An intimate bar and lounge with a full array of beverages complements the dining room.

"Today, Stella Maris is recognized as one of the best places to eat and stay in County Mayo and in Ireland." – **Where to Eat and Stay on the Wild Atlantic Way.**

"Sentinel of the sea on wave-swept Atlantic coast, complete with hand-chiseled gun holes. Glass conservatory for fishbowl views of Bunatrahir Bay."
– **National Geographic Traveler, Best Hotels in Ireland.**

Bedrooms **11**   Hotel ★ ★ ★ ★

Stella Maris Country House Hotel
Ballycastle, Co.Mayo
T +353 (0)96 43322
F +353 (0)96 43965
info@StellaMarisIreland.com
www.StellaMarisIreland.com

Proprietors: Frances Kelly & Terence McSweeney
Open 1 May – 30 September
Wheelchair accessible.
B&B: From €90 – €120 per person sharing.
Single Supplement applies.
Dinner: A la carte menu, 7.00pm – 9.00pm.
Credit cards: MasterCard and Visa.
No service charge. Gratuities at discretion of guests.

How to find:
Stella Maris is located on the ocean 17 miles west of Ballina and 1½ miles west of Ballycastle in Co.Mayo.

GPS coordinates
Lat: 54.29853
Long: -9.39227

A stunning 18th century Georgian house set in 80 acres of magnificent parkland, comprising superbly restored surrounding courtyards and walled gardens. Guests are offered the opportunity to experience genuine hospitality whilst enjoying the true feel of the quintessential Country House.

Situated at the heart of the Boyne Valley in the Heritage county of Meath. Tankardstown is 40 minutes from Dublin City and 30 minutes from Dublin Airport.

Stay in a main house heritage room or in a beautifully appointed court yard cottage. Enjoy simple food in our 'Cellar Restaurant' or more formal dining in our 2AA Rosette Brabazon Restaurant, located in the Tankardstown Garden Village.

AA Guest Accommodation of the Year 2013/2014.
2 **AA** Rosettes for Culinary Excellence.
Lonely Planet's Top 10 Dream Business Destinations 2011.

Bedrooms **7** (main house)   Specialist accommodation **Chic Courtyard Cottages**

Tankardstown House, Nr. Slane, Rathkenny, Co.Meath
T +353 (0)41 982 4621
info@tankardstown.ie
www.tankardstown.ie

Proprietor: Brian & Trish Conroy
Open all year round.
Courtyard Room: €100 – €150 pps B&B
Main House Heritage Bedroom: €315 per room B&B
Master Suite: €350 per room B&B.

How to find:
From Dublin take the M1 motorway and exit at Junction 10. Follow the signs for Slane. Continue straight through the village on N51 — **or**— Take the N2 which will bring you directly into the village of Slane. Turn left at the traffic lights and continue through the village on N51. Come to main entrance gates to Slane Castle on your left. Directly opposite, turn right, at the fork STAY LEFT, and follow straight along this road for 4km. Signposted 'Tankardstown'.

GPS coordinates
N 53° 44' 27"
W 6° 36' 41"

THORNTON'S RESTAURANT

Located right in the centre of Dublin at the top of Dublin's main shopping street – Grafton Street – and overlooking beautiful St Stephen's Green, Thornton's Restaurant occupies the 1st Floor of the 5 Star Fitzwilliam Hotel. A wonderful welcome awaits you in this superb Michelin starred restaurant that has won every major accolade since opening including being listed as Number 25 in the top 50 Restaurants of the World. Kevin Thornton is widely regarded as Ireland's best chef and together with his partner Muriel and the team they look forward to welcoming you.

Thornton's Restaurant,
1st Floor, The Fitzwilliam Hotel,
128 St Stephen's Green, Dublin 2
T +353 (0)1 478 7008 (Reservations)
F +353 (0)1 478 7009
info@thorntonsrestaurant.com

How to find:
We are located on the 1st floor
of the Fitzwilliam Hotel.

Proprietor: Kevin and Muriel Thornton
Open for dinner from 6pm Tuesday to Saturday
and for lunch from 12.30pm Thursday to Saturday.
Lunch from €35.
Dinner Menu €70.
Tasting Menu €90.

Wineport Lodge lakeshore restaurant and luxury hideaway is nestled on the quiet picturesque shores of Lough Ree. Its central location makes this 'hidden gem' easily accessible from anywhere in Ireland, just an hour from Dublin, less from Galway.

The lively buzz of Athlone is within easy reach. Glasson Golf Club is a short boat trip away. The quaint village of Glasson with its traditional pubs, craft shop and gallery is a stroll away. Plus a variety of lakeshore walks start right outside our door.

If you're looking for the ideal hideaway, Wineport Lodge is the perfect place to relax, unwind and revive.

Awards:
The National Hospitality Awards - Best Boutique Hotel in Ireland 2013

Critics quote - *"Dinner is an occasion at Wineport. They take food seriously, putting the same love and care into each dish as they do in creating the perfect retreat for guests."* Julianne Mooney, Travel Writer.

Bedrooms / Suites **29**   Hotel ★ ★ ★ ★

Wineport Lodge, Glasson, Athlone, Co.Westmeath
T +353 (0)90 643 9010
lodge@wineport.ie
www.wineport.ie

Proprietors: Ray Byrne and Jane English
Open all year round.
Closed 24 – 26 December.
Rooms from €69 pps B&B.
Suites from €89 pps B&B.
Early Bird Dinner: €24.95
Table d'Hôte Dinner: €49.
Sunday Lunch (4 course): €37.
Special midweek and weekend breaks available.

How to find:
Take exit 10 off M6/N6 Dublin-Galway.
Follow N55 direction Cavan. At Ballykeeran fork left at Dog & Duck pub. Then 1.6 kilometres (1 mile) on left hand side.

GPS coordinates
N 53.465161
W -7.884579

MARTELLO TOWER SUTTON

Built in 1804, Martello Tower Sutton is located on the north coastline of Dublin Bay, Ireland, with breath-taking views of the Bay and surrounding areas. Set in Red Rock, Sutton, the Tower has been refurbished to a high standard and offers guests a truly unique self catering holiday option as this is the only tower in Ireland available for rental.

Accommodation consists of three levels: two bedrooms and bathroom on the lower level; living area and balcony overlooking the bay on the middle level; and a modern kitchen/dining room offering breathtaking 360° views from roof level.

Martello Tower Sutton offers guests a unique experience, promising a combination of luxury and excitement.

Bedrooms **2**

Martello Tower, Red Rock,
Sutton, Co.Dublin
T +353 (0)86 164 2671
info@martellotowersutton.com

Proprietors: Paul Finnerty & Patricia Muldoon
Pricing is as follows:
For Christmas period pricing is quoted separately.
High season June – August (inclusive)
Min stay 1 week €1,600 please note
arrival Saturday, departure Saturday only.
Low season September – May (inclusive)
Mid week 2 nights €420.
Mid week 3 nights €610.
1 week €1,150.
Weekend €799.
Bank Holiday weekend €975.

How to find:
Martello Tower Sutton is 16km from Dublin Airport and 20km from Dublin City Centre. Detailed directions are available upon request.

PLEASE NOTE: USE OF
THE TOWER FOR A PARTY
VENUE IS NOT PERMITTED.

SCREEBE HOUSE

Located on the wild Atlantic coast of Ireland, this Victorian fishing lodge was built in 1865. A beautiful house, with a large terrace and wonderful landscaped gardens offering a magnificent view over Camus Bay with its own original harbour.

Screebe house has been family owned for many years, which is reflected in the careful attention to detail; all of the rooms are individually furnished with exquisite antique interiors. Whether you are planning a celebration with the family, with friends or business partners, Christmas holidays, birthdays, weddings, christenings or a conference in a peaceful, all fully inclusive of food and beverages for up to 19 guests, or simply want to spend a relaxing holiday amidst unspoilt nature in supreme comfort, Screebe offers the perfect setting.

Bedrooms **9** Suites **1**

Screebe House,
Rosmuc, Connemara, Co.Galway
T +353 (0)91 574 110
info@screebe.com
www.screebe.com

Proprietors: The Burkart Family
Rates: Only available for private hire.

Gym, sauna and swimming pool now available.

How to find:
Screebe is located in Camus Bay, Rosmuc,
Connemara on the R336.
Nearest airports:
Galway (about 40 minutes away)
Knock and Shannon (both about 2 hours away)
Dublin (about 2.5 hours away)
Helicopter landing pad on
Screebe property.

GPS coordinates
N 53.38438
W 9.55539

Sea View House is a luxury holiday home located on the North West coast of Ireland in County Sligo

This peaceful and private hideaway located on Rosses Point offers guests wonderful views of Drumcliff Bay and Benbulben. Sea View is nestled in 14 acres of wild meadow, cleverly hidden away in a sheltered bay with private access to a pebbled beach.

Sea View is the perfect private retreat, promising peace and tranquillity and a blissful escape from the stresses of everyday life. The house is in a secluded & tranquil area but is easily accessed and is within 10 minutes of Sligo town.

Bedrooms **4 double ensuite,** and seperate adjoining fully contained **2 bedroom apartment**

Sea View House, Rosses Lower, Rosses Point, Co.Sligo
T +353 (0)87 2418277
info@seaviewrentals.ie
www.seaviewrentals.ie

Proprietor: John Lyons
Available for private rent all year around.
Rates:
High Season (July & Aug)
€3500 per week....Min 3 nights €2000
Mid Season (May & June)
€3000 per week....Min 3 nights €2000
Low Season (Jan – Apr & Sep – Dec)
€2500 per week....Min 3 nights €2000
Christmas, New Year & Easter weekly €3500
All bedrooms non-smoking.

How to find:
Sea View is 5km from Sligo Town and 16km from Sligo Regional Airport. Detailed directions are available upon request.

DINING WITH THE BLUE BOOK

I started my restaurant in 1964, cooking the food produced on our farms, it was freshly picked, carefully grown, and full of flavour. This is the food of the Irish country houses.
Myrtle Allen, Ballymaloe Country House

The freshest and best of Irish produce, cooked simply, served in great surroundings.
John Mathers, Newforge Country House

Keep it simple.
Frances Kelly, Stella Maris Country House Hotel

Fish is a great Irish resource. My mission is to cook it with care and serve it with style.
Aidan MacManus, King Sitric Restaurant

Use the best and freshest of seasonal produce, cook and present it in a simple and uncomplicated manner.
William O'Callaghan, Longueville House

My philosophy on cooking is to keep it fresh and cook with passion.
Derry Clarke, L'Ecrivain Restaurant

Cooking is a journey of passion and commitment to using the very best products and enhancing their quality.
Ross Lewis, Chapter One Restaurant

At Gregans Castle we produce clear, intense flavours from seasonal produce with a touch of individuality.
Simon Haden, Gregans Castle

The kitchen at The Mustard Seed is influenced by the seasonality of the garden matched with true Irish hospitality at the table.
Dan Mullane, The Mustard Seed

My secret is the finest fish from the day's catch in Youghal Harbour, locally reared beef, seasonal vegetables and local artisan produce.
David Fitzgibbon, Aherne's Townhouse

YOUR SOMETHING BLUE...
IRELAND'S MOST ROMANTIC WEDDING VENUES

Historic Hotels of Europe

www.historichotelsofeurope.com

Austria
Schlosshotels & Herrenhäuser
info@schlosshotels.co.at
www.schlosshotels.co.at

Norway
De Historiske
info@dehistoriske.no
www.dehistoriske.com

Belgium & Netherlands
Hampshire Classic Hotels
info@hampshire-hotels.com
www.hampshire-hotels.com/historic

Poland
Historic Hotels Poland
info@hhpoland.com
www.hhpoland.com

Denmark
Historic Hotels Denmark
info@historichotels.dk
www.historichotels.dk

Portugal
Hotels Heritage Lisboa
heritage.hotels@heritage.pt
www.heritage.pt

France
Symboles de France
contact@symbolesdefrance.com
www.symbolesdefrance.com

Slovakia
Historic Hotels of Slovakia
info@historichotelsofslovakia.com
www.historichotelsofslovakia.com

Greece
Yades Greek Historic Hotels
welcome@yadeshotels.gr
www.yadeshotels.gr

Sweden
Countryside Hotels
info@countrysidehotels.se
www.countrysidehotels.se

Hungary
Hungarian Castle Hotels Association
www.hungariancastlehotels.com
info@hungariancastlehotels.com

Switzerland
Swiss Historic Hotels
info@swiss-historic-hotels.com
www.swiss-historic-hotels.com

Ireland
Ireland's Blue Book
mail@irelandsbluebook.com
www.irelandsbluebook.com

Wales
Welsh Rarebits
info@rarebits.co.uk
www.rarebits.co.uk

Italy
Abitare La Storia
mailbox@abitarelastoria.it
www.abitarelastoria.it

Historic Hotels of Europe
is affiliated with

HISTORIC HOTELS
of AMERICA

NATIONAL TRUST FOR **HISTORIC PRESERVATION**

WELSH RAREBITS ®

Hotels of Distinction

Welsh Rarebits is a unique collection of Wales's best classic and contemporary hotels, chic townhouses, cosy historic inns and top restaurants with rooms.

Pick up a free brochure at your Irish country house hotel/restaurant or contact:
www.rarebits.co.uk /+44 (0) 1570 470785

www.rarebits.co.uk

PORTFOLIO
COLLECTION

WE'VE CHOSEN THE BEST FOR YOU

Personally selected and trusted country houses,
boutique hotels, guest houses,
safari lodges, villas and Bed & Breakfasts
in Southern Africa

Bookings: portfoliocollection.com

Visit our travel blog for stories, reviews and

travel tips:

http://www.portfoliocollection.com/Blogs

HeritageISLAND
IRELAND'S PREMIER ATTRACTIONS

Museums **Historic Houses** Gardens

Distilleries Heritage Towns **Caves**

Interpretative Centres **Family Days Out**

Castles Suggested Tour Itineraries

up to
€500
of discounts

at Ireland's leading
visitor attractions.

Guide available from
www.heritageisland.com

TopAttractions
Ireland.com

**Discount
Pass**

**Visitor
Attractions
Guides**

Info on
What's On

Curators of Style

LIKE SHOPPING. BUT BETTER.

The finest designer boutiques.
All in one place. With up to 60%* off.

ANYA HINDMARCH   BROOKS BROTHERS   CATH KIDSTON

FURLA   JOULES   LINKS OF LONDON   LOUISE KENNEDY

LULU GUINNESS   MOLTON BROWN   AND MANY MORE

KILDARE ✿ VILLAGE
CHIC OUTLET SHOPPING®
KildareVillage.com

EUROPE LONDON DUBLIN PARIS MADRID BARCELONA MILAN BRUSSELS

FRANKFURT MUNICH **CHINA** SUZHOU SHANGHAI (OPENING AUTUMN 2015)

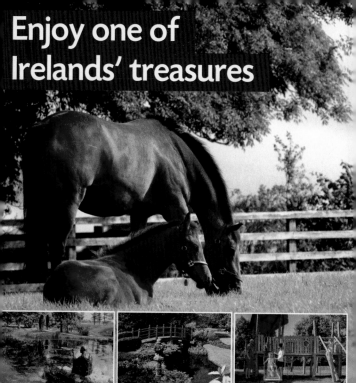

The National Concert Hall of Ireland

The heart of Ireland's music

in the heart of Ireland's capital.

Be sure to drop in before you take off.

Check nch.ie for more details

www.nch.ie
01 417 0000

NATIONAL CONCERT HALL
CEOLÁRAS NÁISIÚNTA

HOUSES CASTLES & GARDENS

OF IRELAND

VISIT • ENJOY • EXPLORE

We can help you:

- ◆ Find delightful heritage properties to visit throughout the island of Ireland
- ◆ Plan excursions for family outings and organised group tours
- ◆ Discover a wide range of events
- ◆ Select beautiful wedding venues for ceremonies, photography and receptions
- ◆ Suggest locations for publicity shoots, TV and feature filming.

Each house or restaurant has a reference number which relates to both the map opposite and the page on which it appears.

1. **Aherne's Townhouse**
   Tel: +353 (0)24 92424
   E-mail: info@ahernes.net

2. **Ardtara Country House & Restaurant**
   Tel: +44 (0)28 796 44490
   From Republic: 048 796 44490
   E-mail: info@ardtara.com

3. **Ballyfin Demesne**
   Tel: +353 (0)57 875 5866
   E-mail: reservations@ballyfin.com

4. **Ballymaloe House**
   Tel: +353 (0)21 465 2531
   E-mail: res@ballymaloe.ie

5. **Barberstown Castle**
   Tel: +353 (0)1 628 8157
   E-mail: info@barberstowncastle.ie

6. **Blairscove Restaurant and Accommodation**
   Tel: +353 (0)27 61127
   E-mail: mail@blairscove.ie

7. **Bushmills Inn**
   Tel: +44 (0)28 207 33000
   From Republic: 048 207 33000
   E-mail: mail@bushmillsinn.com

8. **Campagne Restaurant**
   Tel: +353 (0)56 777 2858
   E-mail: info@campagne.ie

9. **Carrig Country House & Restaurant**
   Tel: +353 (0)66 976 9100
   E-mail: info@carrighouse.com

10. **Cashel House Hotel**
    Tel: +353 (0)95 31001
    E-mail: res@cashel-house-hotel.com

11. **Castle Durrow**
    Tel: +353 (0)57 873 6555
    E-mail: info@castledurrow.com

12. **Castle Leslie Estate**
    Tel: +353 (0)47 88100
    E-mail: info@castleleslie.com

13. **Chapter One Restaurant**
    Tel: +353 (0)1 873 2266
    E-mail: info@chapteronerestaurant.com

14. **Clare Island Lighthouse**
    Tel: +353 (0)87 668 9758
    E-mail: info@clareislandlighthouse.com

15. **Coopershill House**
    Tel: +353 (0)71 916 5108
    E-mail: ohara@coopershill.com

16. **Currarevagh House**
    Tel: +353 (0)91 552312 / 552313
    E-mail: rooms@currarevagh.com

17. **Dunbrody House**
    Tel: +353 (0)51 389600
    E-mail: info@dunbrodyhouse.com

18. **Enniscoe House**
    Tel: +353 (0)96 31112
    E-mail: mail@enniscoe.com

19. **Ghan House**
    Tel: +353 (0)42 937 3682
    E-mail: info@ghanhouse.com

20. **Gregans Castle Hotel**
    Tel: +353 (0)65 707 7005
    E-mail: stay@gregans.ie

21. **Hayfield Manor**
    Tel: +353 (0)21 484 5900
    E-mail: enquiries@hayfieldmanor.ie

22. **Hunter's Hotel**
    Tel: +353 (0)404 40106
    E-mail: reception@hunters.ie

23. **The Ice House**
    Tel: +353 (0)96 23500
    E-mail: chill@theicehouse.ie

24. **King Sitric Fish Restaurant & Accommodation**
    Tel: +353 (0)1 832 5235
    E-mail: info@kingsitric.ie

25. **L'Ecrivain Restaurant**
    Tel: +353 (0)1 661 1919
    E-mail: enquiries@lecrivain.com

26. **Liss Ard Estate**
    Tel: +353 (0)28 40000
    E-mail: reservations@lissardestate.com

27. **Longueville House**
    Tel: +353 (0)22 47156
    E-mail: info@longuevillehouse.ie

28. **Marlfield House**
    Tel: +353 (0)53 94 21124
    E-mail: info@marlfieldhouse.com

29. **Merrion Hotel**
    Tel: +353 (0)1 603 0600
    E-mail: info@merrionhotel.com

30. **Mount Juliet Hotel & Estate**
    Tel: +353 (0)56 777 3000
    E-mail: info@mountjuliet.ie

31. **Moy House**
    Tel: +353 (0)65 708 2800
    E-mail: moyhouse@eircom.net

32. **The Mustard Seed**
    Tel: +353 (0)69 68508
    E-mail: mustard@indigo.ie

33. **Newforge House**
    Tel: +44 (0)28 926 11255
    From Republic: 048 926 11255
    E-mail: enquiries@newforgehouse.com

34. **Newport House**
    Tel: +353 (0)98 41222
    E-mail: info@newporthouse.ie

35. **Park Hotel Kenmare**
    Tel: +353 (0)64 664 1200
    E-mail: info@parkkenmare.com

36. **Rathmullan House**
    Tel: +353 (0)74 915 8188
    E-mail: info@rathmullanhouse.com

37. **Rathsallagh House**
    Tel: +353 (0)45 403112
    E-mail: info@rathsallagh.com

38. **Restaurant Forty One**
    Tel: +353 (0)1 662 0000
    E-mail: info@restaurantfortyone.ie

39. **Restaurant Patrick Guilbaud**
    Tel: +353 (0)1 6764 192
    E-mail: info@restaurantpatrickguilbaud.ie

40. **Rosleague Manor**
    Tel: +353 (0)95 41101
    E-mail: info@rosleague.com

41. **Stella Maris Country House Hotel**
    Tel: +353 (0)96 43322
    E-mail: info@StellaMarisIreland.com

42. **Tankardstown House**
    Tel: +353 (0)41 982 4621
    E-mail: info@tankardstown.ie

43. **Thornton's Restaurant**
    Tel: +353 (0)1 478 7008 (Reservations)
    E-mail: info@thorntonsrestaurant.com

44. **Wineport Lodge**
    Tel: +353 (0)90 643 9010
    E-mail: lodge@wineport.ie

45. **Martello Tower Sutton**
    Tel: +353 (0)86 164 2671
    E-mail: info@martellotowersutton.com

46. **Screebe House**
    Tel: +353 (0)91 574 110
    E-mail: info@screebe.com

47. **Sea View House**
    Tel: +353 (0)87 2418277
    E-mail: info@seaviewrentals.ie